*The Best Things
Ever Said About God*

Other Books Edited by Ronald B. Shwartz

*For the Love of Books: 115 Celebrated Writers
on the Books They Love Most*

Men and Women Talk About Women and Men

What Is Life?

The Best Things Ever Said About God

&

EDITED AND WITH AN INTRODUCTION

BY

Ronald B. Shwartz

Quill

An Imprint of HarperCollins*Publishers*

THE BEST THINGS EVER SAID ABOUT GOD. Copyright © 2000 Ronald B. Shwartz. All rights reserved. Printed in the United States of America. No part of this book may be used or reproduced in any manner whatsoever without written permission except in the case of brief quotations embodied in critical articles and reviews. For information address HarperCollins Publishers Inc., 10 East 53rd Street, New York, NY 10022.

HarperCollins books may be purchased for educational, business, or sales promotional use. For information please write: Special Markets Department, HarperCollins Publishers Inc., 10 East 53rd Street, New York, NY 10022.

FIRST EDITION

Designed by Philip Mazzone

Library of Congress Cataloging-in-Publication Data has been applied for.

ISBN 0–380-80387-2

01 02 03 04 RRD/♋ 10 9 8 7 6 5 4 3 2

To those who believe, to those who don't, to those who take the matter under endless advisement, to those who respectfully could not care less, and to those confused or bemused by the sheer range of options. That about covers it.

Acknowledgments

ಐ

With my thanks to Clarissa Hutton, James Duzak, Dr. Daniel Jacobs, Darline Lewis, and Janet Sutton.

Contents

೮つ

Introduction

&

If the following quotations about God seem incompatible—a fine mess of theology—welcome to my world. I am not an atheist nor, at the other end, have I ever held any religious beliefs at all. At the same time, the term "agnostic" doesn't quite fit either, implying as it does a hedge disguised as intellectual rigor in a realm where logic may be beside the point. As Robert Frost advised, "Don't be agnostic, be *something*"—and something, or at least an *interest* in something larger than ourselves and transcendent—is surely better than nothing. In this regard I once interviewed Frank McCourt of *Angela's Ashes* fame, who said he is obsessed with the notion of faith in God "precisely because I *lack* faith and don't understand it." My own religious outlook, such as it is, mirrors this paradox. It has always been a kind of black hole, conspicuous by its absence, intense but devoid of light. So I've been reading, far and wide—clergy to cranks—in an effort to see the light, or better define the shadows, and grasp where I stand, or at least where others do.

This interest has led, of course, to pundits who wonder if God is indeed the Ultimate Cause or, as Freud said, the ultimate symptom or, as Jung said, the ultimate cure. Unencumbered by studies in history, philosophy, or scripture,

I've read those who risk the stigma of sacrilege by asking if, on balance, the notion of God has bred more good than bad. If more have been saved in God's name than lost to holy wars or stung by guilt or by prayers unanswered. Or preyed on by the likes of Cotton Mather and the Ayatollah Khomeini and latter-day felons posed as televangelists. For all that, I envy the devout. Envy their solace and rapture if not revelation in a secular age—a culture that, for all its addiction to fame, sex, and mutual funds, has run smack into a resurgent interest in spirit and soul. As a recent front-page feature in *The Boston Globe* announced, "From books to TV, the Lord is hot." As if God were just another craze. As if the lure of cosmic truth were a result, according to stale theory, of Baby Boomers in millennial fear of mortality. Like mice in a maze desperate for a big cheese that must be here somewhere, just beyond the hedge.

Maybe, like them, I am best defined by the epithet "neo-agnostics," as coined in a new book called *Working with God*—they are said to be "well-educated skeptics who have metaphysical feelings. They regard religion as belief in the unbelievable, yet sense something important that eludes their most trusted tools of learning and intellect." I guess this kind of muddle fits me as far as it goes but fails to capture the lasting influence of my own religious indoctrination and the metaphysical limbo in which I still find myself adrift. It began with Hebrew School on Long Island, well-meaning but otherwise, if I may say so without slurring the corpus of Talmudic wisdom, daft enough to treat belief in God as a given, *fait accompli*. By failing to start at square one—by showing how to be a Jew but not why—they lost me. Hence the truth told in jest and mock-robotic cadence by another fledgling apostate who never returned to the fold—whose words could almost be my own: "I'm Jewish. I don't really follow the religion. Last time I was in temple, I was thirteen. I made two grand. I got out of the business."

This inquiry of mine has been tantalizing if far from conclusive—and may be the way such things go. Even now, older and ever more apt to contemplate the eternal and my place in a cryptic cosmos, I remain nonsectarian—but not for lack of trying. Rather than "working with God," I have resorted to working on a book *about* God—a book comprised of hearsay at that. It is a miscellany for doubters and believers alike—though at neither extreme—and purged of freeze-dried sermonettes and vainglorious citations to chapter-and-verse as proof that God prefers tea to coffee. A miscellany, that is, for those of open heart and mind who cringe at the first hint of proselytizing. Or at strangers who swear that "God loves you and so do I." Or at prigs without portfolio who dare not laugh at the glib incantations of George Burns in the blockbuster movie, *Oh God!* It is, in short, a collection of the shrewdest, wittiest, and altogether most provocative observations that I have discovered as a pilgrim in progress.

What Is God?

ജ

God is not a cosmic bellboy for whom we can press a button to get things done.

                         so   HARRY EMERSON FOSDICK

God is really only another artist. He invented the giraffe, the elephant and the cat. He has no real style. He just goes on trying other things.

                so   PABLO PICASSO, quoted by Françoise Gilot
                and Carlton Lake, *Life with Picasso*, 1964

God is a sort of burglar. As a young man you knock him down; as an old man you try to conciliate him, because he may knock you down.

                so   SIR H. BEERBOHM-TREE, quoted by
   Hesketh Pearson, *Beerbohm-Tree: His Life and Laughter*, 1956

God is love, but get it in writing.

                         so   GYPSY ROSE LEE

It's God—I'd have known Him by Blake's picture anywhere.

                                                 ɞ   Robert Frost

God is the Celebrity-Author of the World's Best Seller. We have made God into the biggest celebrity of all to contain our own emptiness.

         ɞ   Daniel J. Boorstein, *The Image*, 1962

God is the thought that makes crooked all that is straight.

         ɞ   Friedrich Nietzsche

God is a circle whose center is everywhere and circumference nowhere.

         ɞ   Voltaire, quoting Timaeus of Locris

God is the immemorial refuge of the incompetent, the helpless, the miserable. They find not only sanctuary in His arms, but also a kind of superiority, soothing to their macerated egos; He will set them above their betters.

         ɞ   H. L. Mencken, *Minority Report*, 1956

God, that dumping ground of our dreams.

         ɞ   Jean Rostand, French biologist, *Carnets d'un Biologiste* (*A Biologist's Notebook*), 1962

God help those who don't help themselves.

                                                    ☙ WILSON MIZNER

God was satisfied with his own work, and that is fatal.

                          ☙ SAMUEL BUTLER, *Notebooks*, 1912

God made everything out of nothing, but the nothingness shows through.

             ☙ PAUL VALÉRY, *Mauvaises pensées et autres*, 1942

God has been replaced, as he has all over the West, with respectability and air conditioning.

                        ☙ LEROI JONES, "What Does
Nonviolence Mean?" *Home*, 1966

God may be dead, but fifty thousand social workers have risen to take his place.

                      ☙ J. D. MCCOUGHEY, *Bulletin*, 1974

God—the John Doe of philosophy and religion.

                     ☙ ELBERT HUBBARD, *The Notebook*, 1927

They say that God is everywhere, and yet we always think of Him as somewhat of a recluse.

                                                     ɛœ   EMILY DICKINSON

God is not all that exists; He is all that does not exist.

                                                  ɛœ   RÉMY DE GOURMONT

God, n. 1. A three-letter justification for murder; 2. An unsavory character found in many popular works of fiction, both ancient and modern; 3. An explanation, which means "I have no explanation."

                    ɛœ   ROBERT TEFTON, contemporary American anarchist
and writer, quoted by Charles Bufe,
The Heretics Handbook of Quotations, 1992

God is in the details.

                                  ɛœ   Attributed to architect
LUDWIG MIES VAN DER ROHE

God seems to have left the receiver off the hook and time is running out.

                                    ɛœ   ARTHUR KOESTLER

God is alive and well but working on a much less ambitious project.

> ✍ GRAFFITO, quoted by Patrick Moore in
> *The Observer*, March 18, 1979

God: a disease we imagine we are cured of because no one dies of it nowadays.

> ✍ E. M. CIORAN, Rumanian-born
> French philosopher,
> *The Trouble with Being Born*, 1973

God is the tangential point between zero and infinity.

> ✍ ALFRED JARRY, French playwright and author,
> *Gestes et Opinions du Docteur*
> *Faustroll Pataphysicien*, 1911

God is a concept by which we measure our pain.

> ✍ JOHN LENNON, "God," on the album
> *Plastic Ono Band*, 1970

God is indeed dead.
He died in self-horror
when He saw the creature He had made
in His own image.

> ✍ IRVING LAYTON, Canadian poet,
> *The Whole Bloody Bird*, 1969

God is present whenever a peace treaty is signed.
         ✌ RABBI NAHMAN BEN SIMHA, *The Bratslaver*

God don't make no mistakes—that's how he got to be God.
         ✌ ARCHIE BUNKER from TV's *All in the Family*

The voice which says, "It's not good enough"—that's what God is.
         ✌ WILLIAM ALFRED

I think there are innumerable gods. What we on earth call God is a little tribal God who has made an awful mess.
         ✌ WILLIAM S. BURROUGHS, *Paris Review*, Fall 1965

God: Founder, chairman and CEO of the universe: an invisible boss who readily promotes His more aggressive underlings but has the infinite wisdom to keep them unhappy; neither has He demonstrated undue sympathy toward the meek and the infirm. Has maintained a low profile in recent centuries, apparently preferring to delegate moral authority to military panjandrums, belligerent backwoods preachers, blow-dried TV personalities, politically correct faculty members and other assorted upstarts.
         ✌ RICK BAYAN, *The Cynic's Dictionary*, 1994

God is growing bitter, He envies man his mortality.
         ✌ JACQUES RIGAUT, *Pensées*, c. 1920

God is a verb, not a noun proper or improper.

                                   ɛᴗ   R. BUCKMINSTER FULLER,
No More Secondhand God, 1963
(Also apparently adapted
without attribution by Mary
Daly, *Beyond God the Father*, 1973.)

God is less careful than General Motors, for He floods the world with factory rejects.

ɛᴗ   MIGNON MCLAUGHLIN, *The Complete Neurotic's Notebook*, 1981

God is silent, now if only we can get Man to shut up.

                 ɛᴗ   WOODY ALLEN, "Remembering Needleman," 1976

God provides—if only God would provide until he provides.

                            ɛᴗ   YIDDISH PROVERB

God will forgive me; it is his trade.

                       ɛᴗ   HEINRICH HEINE, last words,
quoted by Alfred Meissner,
Heinrich Heine, Erinnerungen, 1856

God is beginning to resemble not a ruler but the last fading smile of a Cheshire cat.

           ɛᴗ   JULIAN HUXLEY, *Religion Without Revolution*, 1957

God was more exciting then than he is now.

> ❧ Child's comment on the Old Testament,
> quoted by Gerald Kennedy,
> *The Seven Worlds of the Minister*, 1968

God Is Back—and Boy Is He Mad.

> ❧ CALIFORNIA BUMPER STICKER,
> quoted in *Bookviews*, March 1978

God is not what you imagine or what you think you understand.
If you understand you have failed.

> ❧ SAINT AUGUSTINE

God is weak and powerless in the world, and that is precisely
the way, the only way, in which he is with us and helps us. Only
the suffering God can help.

> ❧ DIETRICH BONHOEFFER

God is of no importance unless He is of supreme importance.

> ❧ ABRAHAM JOSHUA HESCHEL, twentieth-century
> American Jewish religious philosopher

It's funny the way some people's name just suits the business
they're in. Like God's name is just *perfect* for God.

> ❧ EDITH BUNKER from TV's *All in the Family*

God is an elderly or, at any rate, middle-aged male, a stern fellow, patriarchal rather than paternal and a great believer in rules and regulations.

        so   P. J. O'ROURKE, *Parliament of Whores*, 1991

God will not look you over for medals, degrees or diplomas, but for scars.

        so   ELBERT HUBBARD, quoted in
Reader's Digest, May 1960

God is an infantile fantasy, which was necessary when men did not understand what lightning was.

        so   EDWARD ANHALT

God is, by definition, ultimate reality. And one cannot argue whether ultimate reality really exists. One can only ask what ultimate reality is like.

        so   J. A. T. ROBINSON, twentieth-century
English Anglican theologian

God is not the name of God, but an opinion about Him.

        so   POPE XYSTUS I, *The Ring*

For me, the single word "God" suggests everything that is slippery, shady, squalid, foul and grotesque.

        ಬಿ   ANDRÉ BRETON

If the concept of God has any validity or any use, it can only be to make us larger, freer, and more loving. If God cannot do this, then it is time to get rid of Him.

        ಬಿ   JAMES BALDWIN

We are all strings in the concert of His job; the spirit from His mouth strikes the note and tune of our strings.

        ಬಿ   JAKOB BOEHME

The world is proof that God is a committee.

        ಬಿ   BOB STOKES

The concept of God has become virtually synonymous with a goodness and a power that transcends us, an elusive, often static spirit beyond our reach, ontologically uninvolved with us.

        ಬಿ   KATIE G. CANNON

The God I believe in is not so fragile that you hurt Him by being angry at Him, or so petty that He will hold it against you for being upset with Him.

        ಬಿ   RABBI HAROLD S. KUSHNER

On the bookshelf of life, God is a useful work of reference, always at hand but seldom consulted.

> ⋙ DAG HAMMARSKJOLD, *Markings*, 1964

The theologians of all ages and races have formed an image of God after their own fancies, and nothing could be more improbable than that He resembles in the least particular their conceptions of Him.

> ⋙ W. MACNEILE DIXON, *The Human Situation*

In making up the character of God, the old theologians failed to mention that He is of infinite cheerfulness. The omission has caused the world much tribulation.

> ⋙ MICHAEL MONAHAN, *Palms of Papyrus*

God is the sum of all possibilities.

> ⋙ ISAAC BASHEVIS SINGER, as quoted in *Reader's Digest*, April 1972

God—but a word invoked to explain the world.

> ⋙ ALPHONS DE LAMARTINE

Clearly, God is a Democrat.

> ⋙ Political pollster PATRICK CADDELL

I love God, and when you get to know Him,
you'll find He's a Livin' Doll.

                                   ઠ   JANE RUSSELL

God is a great humorist. He just has a slow audience to
work with.

                               ઠ   GARRISON KEILLOR

God is a busy worker, but He loves help.

                               ઠ   BASQUE PROVERB

God—the contrapuntal genius of human fate.

                               ઠ   VLADIMIR NABOKOV

God may be subtle, but he isn't mean.

                      ઠ   ALBERT EINSTEIN (Similarly, as
inscribed over a fireplace in Fine Hall,
Princeton, New Jersey, and likewise attributed to
Einstein, "God is clever but not dishonest.")

God: The most popular scapegoat for our sins.

                               ઠ   MARK TWAIN

God was a pretty good novelist; the only trouble was that He was a realist.

> ∾ JOHN BARTH, quoted in
> the *New York Times Book Review*, April 1, 1979

The name of God should no longer come from the mouth of man. This word that has been so long degraded by usage no longer means anything. . . . To use the word God is more than sloth, it's a refusal to think, a kind of short cut, a hideous shorthand.

> ∾ ARTHUR ADAMOV, *The Endless Humiliation*

A perfect God is the creation of a conceited man.

> ∾ SOURCE UNKNOWN

Imagine an artist whose inspiration was ceaseless and continually followed by realization. A Shakespeare or a Beethoven constantly at his best. All we can do to form an idea of God's personality should be in that direction, removing limitations all the time. That is prayer and that is adoration!

> ∾ ERNEST DIMNET, *What We Live By*, 1932

But I always think that the best way to know God is to love many things.

> ∾ VINCENT VAN GOGH,
> *Dear Theo: An Autobiography of Vincent van Gogh*, 1937

I reserve judgment on whether God is a conservative or not.

      ᔐ   JOHN KENNETH GALBRAITH, as quoted in *Life*, Jan. 1982

God is a gaseous vertebrate.

      ᔐ   ERNST HAECKEL

God and other artists are always a little obscure.

      ᔐ   OSCAR WILDE, to Ada Leverson, Dec. 1894

"God" is a word, however problematical, we do not have to look up in the dictionary. We seem to have its acquaintance from birth.

      ᔐ   JOHN UPDIKE, *Self-Consciousness: Memoirs*, 1989

God is being itself, not *a* being.

      ᔐ   PAUL TILLICH

The biggest problem I face while teaching is convincing the preschoolers that Barney is not God.

      ᔐ   ROBERT G. LEE

"God is Love," we are taught as children to believe. But when we first begin to get some inkling of how He loves us, we are repelled; it seems so cold, indeed, not love at all as we understand the word.

          ဆ   W. H. AUDEN, *A Certain World*, 1970

It is easy to know God so long as you do not tax yourself with defining Him.

          ဆ   JOSEPH JOUBERT

The way God has been thought of for thousands of years is no longer convincing; if anything is dead, it can only be the traditional *thought* of God.

          ဆ   HANNA ARENDT

God is always more unlike what we say than like it.

          ဆ   DENISE LARDNER CARMODY

A man, asked to explain what God is, replied, "I know if I'm not asked."

          ဆ   ANONYMOUS

To the lexicographer, God is simply the word that goes next to go-cart.

                                              ℰ   SAMUEL BUTLER

We can know what God is not, but we cannot know what He is.

                                            ℰ   SAINT AUGUSTINE

The only God worth talking about is a God that cannot be talked about.

                                            ℰ   WALTER KAUFMANN

Does God Exist?

෴

I guess I began to doubt the existence of God after I had been married for about three years.

                                            ✆   BRIAN SAVAGE

How can I believe in God when just last week I got my tongue caught in the roller of an electric typewriter?

                        ✆   WOODY ALLEN, "Selections from the Allen Notebooks," *Without Feathers*, 1975

I don't believe in God because I don't believe in Mother Goose.

                   ✆   CLARENCE DARROW, speech in Toronto, 1930

I do not believe in God. I believe in cashmere.

                                       ✆   FRAN LEBOWITZ

The idea of a Supreme Being who creates a world in which one creature is designed to eat another in order to subsist, and then pass a law saying "thou shalt not kill," is so monstrously, immeasurably, bottomlessly absurd that I am at a loss to understand how mankind has entertained or given it house room all this long.

           ℘   PETER DE VRIES

It is an insult to God to believe in God. For on the one hand it is to suppose that he has perpetrated acts of incalculable cruelty. On the other hand, it is to suppose that he has perversely given his human creatures an instrument—their intellect—which must inevitably lead them, if they are dispassionate and honest, to deny his existence. It is tempting to conclude that if he exists, it is the atheists and agnostics that he loves best, among those with any pretensions to education. For they are the ones who have taken him most seriously.

           ℘   GALEN STRAWSON, British philosopher and critic, quoted in *Independent*, June 24, 1990

Some people want an affidavit from God that He really exists.

           ℘   Actor/Comedian DANNY THOMAS, quoted in *Reader's Digest*, July 1955

God can stand being told by Professor Ayer and Marghanita Laski that He doesn't exist.

           ℘   J. B. PRIESTLY, in *Listener*, July 1, 1965

I cannot believe in a God who wants to be praised all the time.

> ∞ FRIEDRICH NIETZSCHE

We've never been intimate.

> ∞ NOËL COWARD, on being asked if he believed in God, in interview with David Frost, 1969

I know not which is the more childish—to deny God, or to define Him.

> ∞ SAMUEL BUTLER

It's an interesting view of atheism, as a sort of *crutch* for those who can't stand the reality of God.

> ∞ TOM STOPPARD

God does not believe in our God.

> ∞ JULES RENARD

I respect the idea of God too much to hold it responsible for a world as absurd as this one is.

> ∞ GEORGES DUHAMEL, *Le Desert de Bievres*, 1937

Polite society believed in God so that it need not talk of Him.

> ∞ JEAN-PAUL SARTRE, *Words*, 1946

Why should He hide Himself in the midst of half-spoken promises and unseen miracles? Why can't I kill God within me? Why does He live on in this painful and humiliating way even though I curse Him and want to tear Him out of my heart?

> ∞ MAX VON SYDOW, in an internal struggle, trying to rid himself of a belief in a merciful God, in the 1957 film *The Seventh Seal*

God is a luxury I cannot afford.

> ∞ MARTIN LANDAU, explaining to a rabbi that, if he were to believe in God, he could not live with the fact that he is responsible for the murder of his mistress, in the 1989 film *Crimes and Misdemeanors*

No matter how much I prove and prod,
I cannot quite believe in God;
But oh, I hope to God that He
Unswervingly believes in me.

> ∞ Limerick attributed to E. Y. HARBURG

People see God every day, they just don't recognize him.

> ∞ PEARL BAILY, quoted in the *New York Times*, Nov. 26, 1967

I know absolutely nothing about God. I have always lived, you see, in one of the rural districts of the universe.

> ∞ ROBERT INGERSOLL, quoted in *Ingersoll the Magnificent*, 1983

People are too apt to treat God as if he were a minor royalty.
> ଛ   SIR HERBERT BEERBOHM-TREE
> English actor-manager,
> quoted by Hesketh Pearson, *Beerbohm-Tree*, 1956

We treat God as the police treat a man when he has been arrested; whatever He does will be used in evidence against Him.
> ଛ   C. S. LEWIS, *Essays on Theology and Ethics*,
> ed. Walter Hooper, 1970

One of the silliest of all discussions is the question whether God is personal—it would be more useful to inquire whether ice is frozen.
> ଛ   AUSTIN FARRER, Warden, Keble College,
> Oxford, *Saving Belief*, 1964

I took this form because if I showed myself to you as I am, you wouldn't be able to comprehend me.
> ଛ   GEORGE BURNS, as God,
> in the 1977 film *Oh, God*

I saw the face of God!
> ଛ   MITCHELL GREENBERG, in the 1985 film *Insignificance*, standing
> beneath the subway grill where Marilyn Monroe–like actress
> Theresa Russell stands as her white dress billows up over
> her head in the famous sequence from *The Seven Year Itch*

To attribute existence to God is the most extreme form of anthropomorphism.

           ℵ   LESLIE DEWART

A God who let us prove his existence would be an idol.

      ℵ   DIETRICH BONHOEFFER, *No Rusty Swords*, 1965

If God didn't exist, it would be necessary to invent him.

      ℵ   VOLTAIRE, *Letters*, vol. xcvi, 1769
(As elaborated by Albert Camus:
If God did not exist, we should have to invent him.
If God did exist, we should have to abolish him.)

Finding God in the history of the holocaust will help us come across Him in our private hells and holocausts. A religiosity which does not address itself to such tasks is slop!

      ℵ   LIONEL BLUE and JONATHAN MAGONET

The only excuse for God is that he doesn't exist.

      ℵ   STENDHAL (MARIE HENRI BEYLE)

Not only is there no God, but try getting a plumber on weekends.

      ℵ   WOODY ALLEN, "My Philosophy,"
The New Yorker, Dec. 27, 1969

It is as impossible for man to demonstrate the existence of God as it would be for even Sherlock Holmes to demonstrate the existence of Arthur Conan Doyle.

ဢ FREDERICK BUECHNER,
Wishful Thinking: A Theological ABC, 1973

The very impossibility in which I find myself to prove that God is not, discloses to me His existence.

ဢ JEAN DE LA BRUYÈRE

Our only hope rests on the off-chance that God does exist.

ဢ ALICE THOMAS ELLIS, *Unexplained Laughter*, 1985

Intelligence, I admit, is no safeguard if one is determined to leap into disbelief.

ဢ BARBARA HARRISON

It is the final proof of God's omnipotence that he need not exist in order to save us.

ဢ PETER DE VRIES, *The Mackerel Plaza*, 1958

That God has managed to survive the inanities of the religions that do Him homage is truly a miraculous proof of His existence.

ဢ BEN HECHT

I could prove God statistically. Take the human body alone—the chances that all the functions of an individual would just happen is a statistical monstrosity.

         ∞   GEORGE GALLUP

The atheist who seriously studies religion in order to attack it is closer to the spirit of God than the bovine believer who supports religion because it is comfortable, respectable, and offers consolation without thought. If God's greatest gift to men is reason, then refusing to exercise reason is the greatest impiety.

         ∞   SYDNEY J. HARRIS

By night an atheist half believes in God.

         ∞   EDWARD YOUNG, *Night Thoughts*, 1820

My atheism, like that of Spinoza, is true piety towards the universe and denies only gods fashioned by men in their own image to be servants of their human interests.

         ∞   GEORGE SANTAYANA

The worst moment for the athiest is when he is really thankful and has nobody to thank.

         ∞   DANTE GABRIEL ROSSETTI

An atheist is a man who believes himself an accident.
>> Francis Thompson, *Paganism Old and New*

An atheist is a man who has no invisible means of support.
>> John Buchan, Lord Tweedsmuir

Sometimes I think we're alone. Sometimes I think we're not. In either case, the thought is quite staggering.
>> R. Buckminster Fuller, quoted in *Omni*, April 1980

Atheists have an excellent longevity record because we have no place to go after we die, so we take good care of ourselves and our world while we are here.
>> Madalyn Murray O'Hair, famous atheist

An atheist is a guy who watches a Notre Dame–SMU game and doesn't care who wins.
>> Dwight D. Eisenhower

A young man who wishes to remain a sound atheist cannot be too careful of his reading. God is, if I may say it, very unscrupulous.
>> C. S. Lewis, quoted in the *New York Times*, Dec. 20, 1976

There's something in every atheist, itching to believe, and something in every believer, itching to doubt.

                                         ১ MIGNON MCLAUGHLIN,
The Complete Neurotic's Notebook, 1981

To you I'm an atheist, to God I'm the loyal opposition.

                                  ১ WOODY ALLEN, in the 1980 movie
Stardust Memories, responding to a studio
executive who calls him an atheist

A dead atheist is someone who's all dressed up
with no place to go.

                 ১ JAMES DUFFECY, quoted in the *New York Times*, 1964

If there is a God, atheism must seem to Him as less an insult
than religion.

                               ১ EDMOND AND JULES DE GONCOURT

The atheists have produced a Christmas play. It's called
Coincidence on 34th Street.

                                            ১ JAY LENO

Basically I think it is stupid not to believe in God.

                                   ১ EUGENE IONESCO, quoted in
Harvard Magazine, Nov. 24, 1986

I am a born-again atheist.

                                                          ∞   Gore Vidal

Looking for loopholes.

            ∞   W. C. Fields, an atheist his entire life, asked on
                      his deathbed why he was reading the Bible

There can be no Creator, simply because his grief at the fate of
his creation would be inconceivable and unendurable.

            ∞   Elias Canetti, *The Human Province*, 1978

Agnosticism simply means that a man shall not say he knows or
believes that for which he has no grounds for professing to
believe.

            ∞   Thomas Henry Huxley

Don't be agnostic—be something.

            ∞   Robert Frost

I am an agnostic. I do not pretend to know what many ignorant
men are sure of.

            ∞   Clarence Darrow

If you cross an agnostic with a Jehovah's Witness, you get a fellow who knocks on your door for no particular reason.

          ℬ   BLANCHE KNOTT

Experience has repeatedly confirmed that well-known maxim of [Francis] Bacon's that "a little philosophy inclineth a man's mind to atheism, but depth in philosophy bringeth men's minds about to religion." At the same time, when Bacon penned that sage epigram . . . he forgot to add that the God to whom depth in philosophy brings back men's minds is far from being the same from whom a little philosophy estranges them.

          ℬ   GEORGE SANTAYANA

If God is dead, as some now say, he no doubt died of trying to find an equitable solution to the Arab-Jewish problem.

          ℬ   I. F. STONE

God is everywhere, even though we can't see Him. He's the one who opens the doors at the supermarkets.

          ℬ   GEORGE ANDERSON

I cannot conceive of a God who rewards and punishes his creatures, or has a will of the kind that we experience in ourselves.

          ℬ   ALBERT EINSTEIN, *Ideas and Opinions*, 1954

Many years ago, when Harry was five or thereabouts, William undertook to explain to him the nature of God, and hearing that he was everywhere, asked whether he was the chair or the table. "Oh, no! God isn't a thing; He is everywhere about us; He pervades." "Oh, then, he is a skunk." How would the word "pervade" suggest anything else to an American child?

                ⅏   ALICE ADAMS, *The Diary of Alice Adams*

I don't know if God exists, but it would be better for His reputation if he didn't.

                ⅏   JULES RENARD

I turned to speak to God
    about the world's despair;
    but to make matters worse
    I found God wasn't there.

                ⅏   ROBERT FROST, "Not All There"

If you gain, you gain all; if you lose, you lose nothing. Wager, then, without hesitation, that He exists.

                ⅏   BLAISE PASCAL

God's only excuse is that he does not exist.

                ⅏   STENDHAL (MARIE HENRI BEYLE),
                     quoted by Nietzsche in *Ecce Homo*, 1888

If God exists, why write literature? And if He doesn't, why write literature?

>   ‖   EUGÈNE IONESCO, *Non*, 1934

After one has abandoned a belief in God, poetry is that essence which takes its place as life's redemption.

>   ‖   WALLACE STEVENS, *Opus Posthumous*, 1957

God [or believing in God] is a convenient way of expressing our wonder in the vast splendor of the universe, and our humility over the modesty of man's achievements.

>   ‖   BROOKS ATKINSON

To believe in God is impossible—not to believe in Him is absurd.

>   ‖   VOLTAIRE

I would believe only in a God that knows how to dance.

>   ‖   FRIEDRICH NIETZSCHE

It is difficult to believe in God, not because He is so far off, but because He is so near.

>   ‖   MARK RUTHERFORD, *Last Pages from a Journal*

Once you accept the existence of God—however you define him, however you explain your relationship to him—then you are caught forever with his presence in the center of all things.

           ဆ   Morris West, *The Clowns of God*, 1981

I have some obsession with how God exists. Is He an essential god or an existential god; is He all-powerful or is He, too, an embattled existential creature who may succeed or fail in His vision?

           ဆ   Norman Mailer, interview in
Writers at Work, ed. George Plimpton, 1967

An atheist may be simply one whose faith and love are concentrated on the impersonal aspects of God.

           ဆ   Simone Weil

If you want to find God, stop looking for Him.

           ဆ   Brendan Francis

We dance round in a ring and suppose,
But the Secret sits in the middle and knows.

           ဆ   Robert Frost, couplet from his collection
In the Clearing, 1962

To stand on one leg and prove God's existence is a very different thing from going down on one's knees and thanking him.

            ဆ   SØREN KIERKEGAARD

I simply haven't the nerve to imagine a being, a force, a cause
which keeps the planets revolving in their orbits, and then suddenly stops in order to give me a bicycle with three speeds.

             ဆ   QUENTIN CRISP

I've always regarded nature as the clothing of God.

             ဆ   ALAN HOVHANESS

The believer in God must explain one thing, the existence of
suffering; the nonbeliever, however, must explain the existence
of everything else.

        ဆ   DENNIS PRAGER and JOSEPH TELUSHKIN,
        The Nine Questions People Ask About Judaism, 1981

Some people talk about finding God—as if He could get lost.

             ဆ   ANONYMOUS

If a universal mind does in fact exist, then we must be willing to
accept the possibility of its insanity.

          ဆ   Attributed to DAMON KNIGHT,
           in *The Village Voice*, Aug. 21, 1978

God is more truly imagined than expressed, and he exists more truly than he is imagined.

                                 SAINT AUGUSTINE, *De Trinitate*

If it represents progress to believe in one God rather than many, why not take the next step?

                                 MICHEL PAUL RICHARD

I do not believe in God, for that implies an effort of the will—I see God everywhere!

                                 JEAN FAVRE

Atheism is the folly of the metaphysician, not the folly of human nature.

                                 GEORGE BANCROFT

An atheist is a man who looks through a telescope and tries to explain what he can't see.

                     O. A. BATTISTA, *Power to Influence People*, 1959

Atheism is a theoretical formulation of the discouraged life.

                            HARRY EMERSON FOSDICK

To ask for proof of the existence of God is on a par with asking for proof of the existence of beauty.

                           ᔕ   WALTER T. STACE

It may be, as some extreme saints have implied, that beneath the majesty of the infinite, believers and non-believers are exactly alike.

                           ᔕ   JOHN UPDIKE

The best reply to an atheist is to give a good dinner and ask if he believes there is a cook.

                           ᔕ   LOUIS NIZER

I have encountered nothing on *Apollo* 15 or in this age of space and science that dilutes my faith in God. While I was on the moon, in fact, I felt a sense of inspiration, a feeling that someone was with me and watching over me, protecting me. There were several times when tasks seemed to be impossible—but they worked out all right every time.

                   ᔕ   COLONEL JAMES B. IRWIN,
as quoted in the *New York Times*, Aug. 13, 1971

No one has ever died an atheist.

                           ᔕ   PLATO, *Laws*, X

Atheists brag that they can get along without God; this is hardly a distinction in an era where very, very few pay the Lord more than a Sunday call.

                  &so;   DAGOBERT D. RUNES, *Dictionary of Thought*, 1959

I admit that the generation which produced Stalin, Auschwitz and Hiroshima will take some beating; but the radical and universal consciousness of the death of God is still ahead of us; perhaps we shall have to colonize the stars before it is finally borne in upon us that God is not out there.

                  &so;   R. J. HOLLINGDALE, British author and critic,
Thomas Mann: A Critical Study, 1971

Q: What's the only thing wrong with being an atheist?
A: Nobody to talk to during an orgasm.

                  &so;   SOURCE UNKNOWN

If the work of God could be comprehended by reason, it would be no longer wonderful.

                  &so;   POPE GREGORY I
Saint Gregory the Great

I cannot imagine how the clockwork of the universe can exist without a clockmaker.

                  &so;   VOLTAIRE

"I was six when I saw that everything was God, and my hair stood up, and all," Teddy said. "It was on a Sunday, I remember. My sister was a tiny child then, and she was drinking her milk, and all of a sudden I saw that she was God and the milk was God. I mean, all she was doing was pouring God into God, if you know what I mean."

ဢ   "TEDDY" in J. D. Salinger's short story of the same name, 1954

What God Does

৪৩

I am always humbled by the infinite ingenuity of the lord, who can make a red barn cast a blue shadow.

                                                        ∞   E. B. WHITE

The good Lord never gives you more than you can handle. Unless you die of something.

                                       ∞   GUINDON cartoon caption

The only thing that stops God from sending a second Flood is that the first one was useless.

                                    ∞   NICOLAS CHAMFORT
Characters and Anecdotes, 1771

If there were no other proof of the infinite patience of God with men, a very good one could be found in His toleration of the pictures that are painted of Him and of the noise that proceeds from musical instruments under the pretext of being in His "honor."

                         ∞   THOMAS MERTON, in *The Commonweal
Reader*, ed. E. S. Skillin, 1950

Despair is only the symptom; God knows what the disease is.

                    ✍ MIGNON MCLAUGHLIN,
             The Complete Neurotic's Notebook, 1981

God must have loved the plain people; he made so
many of them.

                          ✍ ABRAHAM LINCOLN

God doesn't make orange juice; God makes oranges.

                           ✍ JESSE JACKSON

God shows his contempt for wealth by the kind of person he
selects to receive it.

                       ✍ AUSTIN O'MALLEY

God gives the milk but not the pail.

                         ✍ ENGLISH PROVERB

God doesn't make any losers.

                ✍ TOM LANDRY, professional football coach,
           quoted in the *Chicago Sun-Times*, April 21, 1979

Russia has abolished God, but so far God has been
more tolerant.

            ℘   JOHN CAMERON SWAYZE, quoted in
                             Reader's Digest, July 1959

I think it pisses God off if you walk by the color purple in a
field somewhere and don't take notice.

            ℘   ALICE WALKER, *The Color Purple*, 1982

God casts the die, not the dice.

            ℘   ALBERT EINSTEIN (Also by Einstein:
             "God does not play dice with the universe.")

God plays dice with the universe. But they're loaded dice. And
the main objective is to find out by what rules they were loaded
and how we can use them for our own ends.

            ℘   JOSEPH FORD, quoted by James Gleick,
             Chaos: Making a New Science, 1987

God seems to have an inordinate fondness for beetles.

            ℘   J. B. S. HALDANE, British scientist

Why attack God? He may be as miserable as we are.

            ℘   ERIK SATIE, quoted by John Gross,
             The Oxford Book of Aphorisms, 1983

The world is more exacting than God himself.

                                                YIDDISH PROVERB

When something good happens, it's a miracle, and you should wonder what God is saving up for you later.

                                    MARSHALL BRICKMAN

I think God invented rain to give dead people something to complain about.

                                           DAVID BRENNER

God always has another custard pie up his sleeve.

                                LYNN REDGRAVE in the
                                Broadway play *Georgy Girl*

Never forget that [God] tests his real friends more severely than the lukewarm ones.

                              KATHRYN HULME, *The Nun's Story*

God will send the bill to you.

                                  JAMES RUSSELL LOWELL

Sometimes I wonder whose side God's on.

                                JOHN WAYNE in the 1962 film
                                The Longest Day

The issue is not what God is like. The issue is what kind of people we become when we attach ourselves to God.

        ဏ   RABBI HAROLD S. KUSHNER

No matter how much we may like to pussyfoot around it, all of us who postulate a loving God eventually come to a single terrifying idea: God wants us to become Himself (or Herself or itself). We are growing toward godhood. God is the goal of evolution.

        ဏ   M. SCOTT PECK

God has a history of using the insignificant to accomplish the impossible.

        ဏ   attributed to RICHARD EXLEY, in
God's Little Instruction Book II, 1994

God made pot. Man made beer. Who do you trust?

        ဏ   GRAFFITO, reported in the *Irish Times*,
Washington, D.C., 1995[?]

I am the vessel. The draft is God's. And God is the thirsty one.

        ဏ   DAG HAMMARSKJOLD, *Markings*, 1964

There are two kinds of people: those who say to God, "Thy will be done," and those to whom God says, "All right, then, have it your way."

             ℅   C. S. LEWIS, *The Screwtape Letters*, 1943

Did God who gave us flowers and trees,/ Also provide the allergies?

            ℅   E. Y. HARBURG, "A Nose Is a Nose Is a Nose," 1965

A blank page is God's way of telling you how hard it is being God.

                            ℅   ANONYMOUS

Cocaine is God's way of telling you, you have too much money.

                         ℅   ROBIN WILLIAMS

I think war might be God's way of teaching us geography.

                            ℅   PAUL RODRIGUEZ

A baby is God's opinion that the world should go on.

  ℅   CARL SANDBURG, quoted in the *Kansas City Star*, Feb. 20, 1977

Conceit is God's gift to little men.

               ℅   BRUCE BARTON, *Coronet*, Sept. 1958

An earthquake is God grabbing the earth and saying, "Cough."

                                                         so RICHARD BELZER

Life is God's novel. Let him write it.

                           so ISAAC BASHEVIS SINGER,
quoted by Dom Moraes, ed., *Voices for Life*, 1975

Impotence is God's way of keeping a man in touch with his feelings. [But even God could not have contemplated we would have created a world that condemned men for their powerlessness to such an extent that they would forget what a soft penis is for.]

                             so DR. WARREN FARRELL,
Why Men Are the Way They Are, 1986

God made death so we'd know when to stop.

                                    so STEVEN STILES

Extinction is God's way of letting a species know it no longer has a job description.

           so ADAM CLATSOFF, Florida talk show host, quoted in *Daily Business Review*, May 27, 1995

Gray hair is God's graffiti.

                                    so BILL COSBY

A coincidence is a small miracle where God prefers to remain anonymous.

                        ৪০   SOURCE UNKNOWN

If God is testing us, why doesn't He give us a written?

          ৪০   WOODY ALLEN in the 1975 film *Love and Death*

If God made us in his image, we have more than returned the compliment.

                    ৪০   VOLTAIRE, *Le Sottisier*

One of the most annoying things about God is that he never just touches you with his magic wand, like Glinda the Good, and gives you what you want. Like it would be so much skin off his nose.

                         ৪০   ANNE LAMOTT

As Kurt Vonnegut once said in the epigraph of an early novel, the innocent don't need protection because "God Almighty protects the innocent as a matter of Heavenly routine."

      ৪০   TIM ALLEN, *Don't Stand Too Close to a Naked Man*, 1994

If God wanted us to be brave, why did He give us legs?

             ∞   MARVIN KITMAN

If God had intended us to fly he would never have given us railways.

      ∞   MICHAEL FLANDERS, the *New York Times*, April 16, 1975

If God's got anything better than sex to offer, he's certainly keeping it to himself.

              ∞   STING

If God were suddenly condemned to live the life which he has inflicted upon men, he would kill himself.

      ∞   ALEXANDRE DUMAS FILS, *Pensées d'album*

If God wanted us to vote, he would have given us candidates.

             ∞   JAY LENO

If God had been a Liberal there wouldn't have been Ten Commandments, there would have been Ten Suggestions.

      ∞   MALCOLM BRADBURY, *After Dinner Game*, 1982

If only God would give me some clear sign! Like making a large deposit in my name at a Swiss bank.

                                                     ଚ   WOODY ALLEN

God will provide—ah, if only He would till He does!

                                                     ଚ   YIDDISH PROVERB

God gives nuts to the toothless.

                                                     ଚ   SPANISH PROVERB

God laughs because He knows more than we do. God has sharper vision.

                                                 ଚ   MIRIAM POLLARD

God has more than He has given away.

                                                   ଚ   CZECH PROVERB

Every day God makes silk purses out of sows' ears.

                                                   ଚ   SOURCE UNKNOWN

God favors those who have nothing to say and who can't be persuaded to say.

                                                   ଚ   JEWISH SAYING

God is closest to those with broken hearts.

                                                  ℘   JEWISH SAYING

When God wants to break a man's heart, he gives him a lot of sense.

                                                  ℘   JEWISH SAYING

God offers to every mind its choice between truth and repose. Take which you please; you can never have both.

                                 ℘   RALPH WALDO EMERSON

The Lord may not come when you want him, but he's always going to be there on time.

                                       ℘   LOU GOSSETT, JR.

God gave burdens, also shoulders.

                                         ℘   YIDDISH PROVERB

When God shuts one door, He opens another.

                                         ℘   IRISH PROVERB

God's mill grinds slow, but it grinds exceedingly fine.

                                         ℘   GERMAN PROVERB

God does not pay by the week, but he pays at the end.

                                     ട   DUTCH PROVERB

If God had meant for everything to happen at once, he would not have invented desk calendars.

              ട   FRAN LEBOWITZ, *Time*, May 29, 1978

If God doesn't destroy Hollywood Boulevard, he owes Sodom and Gomorrah an apology.

                                         ട   JAY LENO

The word of the Lord falls with the force of a snowflake.

                     ട   REV. WILLIAM SLOANE COFFIN

The finger of God never leaves identical fingerprints.

                            ട   STANISLAUS LEC

So long as God reveals Himself, or doesn't, He is behaving like God.

                           ട   MIGNON MCLAUGHLIN,
The Complete Neurotic's Notebook, 1981

The Lord loveth a cheerful giver. He also accepteth from a grouch.

                            ട   CATHERINE HALL

God often visits us, but most of the time we are not at home.

      ໄ   JOSEPH ROUX, *Meditations of a Parish Priest*, 1886

All sentences that start with "God forbid" describe what is possible.

                                        ໄ   JEWISH SAYING

The very contradictions in my life are in some ways signs of God's mercy to me.

                ໄ   THOMAS MERTON, Preface to
The Thomas Merton Reader, 1962

When suffering comes, we yearn for some sign from God, forgetting we have just had one.

ໄ   MIGNON MCLAUGHLIN, *The Complete Neurotic's Notebook*, 1981

God pays well, but He is often in arrears.

    ໄ   Quoted from *Leo Rosten's Treasury of Jewish Quotations*, 1977

Our dream dashes itself against the great mystery like a wasp against a window pane. Less merciful than man, God never opens the window.

                  ໄ   JULES RENARD, *Journal*, 1906

God protect us from our friends. Our enemies, we can handle by ourselves.

                                            ∽   JEWISH SAYING

In general, God is perpetually creating us, that is, developing our real manhood, our spiritual reality. Like a good teacher, He is engaged in detaching us from a false dependence upon Him.

                  ∽   CHARLES SANDERS PIERCE, *Collected Papers of Charles Sanders Pierce*, Vol. VI

God made man. God made woman. And when God found that men could not get along with women, God invented Mexico.

                                       ∽   LARRY STORCH

God enters by a private door into each individual.

                                 ∽   RALPH WALDO EMERSON

If you're caught on a golf course during a storm and are afraid of lightning, hold up a 1-iron. Not even God can hit a 1-iron.

                         ∽   LEE TREVINO, on *The Tonight Show*, Jan. 1985

If God meant for us to travel tourist class he would have made us narrower.

                      ∽   Airline hostess MARTHA ZIMMERMAN, as quoted in the *Wall Street Journal*, 1977

God gives nothing to those who keep their arms crossed.

> ℘   WEST AFRICAN SAYING

Einstein was a man who could ask immensely simple questions. And what his work showed is that when the answers are simple, too, then you can hear God thinking.

> ℘   JACOB BRONOWSKI

God can heal a broken heart, but He has to have all the pieces.

> ℘   SOURCE UNKNOWN

God loves you and I'm trying.

> ℘   BUMPER STICKER

God made the world round so we would never be able to see too far down the road.

> ℘   ISAK DINESEN, recalled on her death,
> Sept. 7, 1962

We need to talk.

> ℘   GOD, purportedly quoted on a billboard conceived by
> advertising executive Charlie Robb of the
> Smith Agency in Fort Lauderdale, Florida

God and Religion

દ

Every day people are straying away from the church and going back to God. Really.

                               ဆ   LENNY BRUCE, "Religions Inc.,"
in The Essential Lenny Bruce, ed. John Cohen, 1967

Most sermons sound to me like commercials—but I can't make out whether God is the Sponsor or the Product.

                               ဆ   MIGNON MCLAUGHLIN,
The Complete Neurotic's Notebook, 1981

Religion is the work of God, perfected by the Devil.

                               ဆ   PETER USTINOV

Grace is God taking you out for a milkshake after a baseball game whether you go 3 for 4 or 0 for 5.

                               ဆ   SOURCE UNKNOWN

In general, the churches, visited by me often on weekdays . . .
bore for me the same relation to God that billboards did to
Coca-Cola; they promoted thirst without quenching it.

      ɛ∂ JOHN UPDIKE, *A Month of Sundays*, 1975

My religious position: I think that God could do a lot better, and
I'm willing to give Him the chance.

       ɛ∂ MIGNON MCLAUGHLIN,
       The Complete Neurotic's Notebook, 1981

All your Western theologies, the whole mythology of them, are
based on the concept of God as a senile delinquent.

     ɛ∂ TENNESSEE WILLIAMS, *The Night of the Iguana*, 1961

I don't know why it is that the religious never ascribe common
sense to God.

     ɛ∂ W. SOMERSET MAUGHAM, *A Writer's Notebook*, 1949

The point is, could God pass an examination in Theology?

      ɛ∂ MALCOLM MUGGERIDGE

Religion is more than a fire insurance policy.

       ɛ∂ SOURCE UNKNOWN

We use religion like a trolley-car—we ride on it only while it is going our way.

                                                 ≈   SOURCE UNKNOWN

The whole religious experience of the modern world is due to the absence from Jerusalem of a lunatic asylum.

                                               ≈   HAVELOCK ELLIS

Men will wrangle for religion; write for it; fight for it; die for it; anything but *live* for it.

                                               ≈   CHARLES COLTON

It is the test of a good religion whether you can joke about it.

                                               ≈   G. K. CHESTERTON

So far as religion of the day is concerned, it is a damned fake. . . . Religion is all bunk.

                                               ≈   THOMAS EDISON

It is inconceivable that religion may be morally useful without being intellectually sustainable.

                                               ≈   JOHN STUART MILL

One man's religion is another man's belly laugh

> ഗ ROB SHERMAN, quoted in
> *Chicago Tribune Magazine*, Aug. 8, 1993

A wise man once said that the only difference between a cult and a religion is the amount of real estate they own.

> ഗ FRANK ZAPPA, quoted in
> *National Catholic Reporter*, Aug. 14, 1987

It is a fine thing to establish one's own religion in one's heart, not to be dependent on tradition and second-hand ideals. Life will seem to you, later, not a lesser, but a greater thing.

> ഗ D. H. LAWRENCE, *Selected Letters of D. H. Lawrence*, 1958

What a travesty to think religion means saving my little soul through my little good deeds and the rest of the world go hang.

> ഗ GERALD VANN, *The Heart of Man*, 1944

I believe it would be healthier if the church could laugh because I believe that God laughs.

> ഗ REV. FLOYD SCHAFFER, as quoted in
> *Newsweek*, Sept. 29, 1975

In religion, our inclusions are nearly always wrong, and our exclusions, however inconsistent, nearly always right.

> ഗ EVELYN UNDERHILL, *The Letters of Evelyn Underhill*, 1989

I have treated many hundreds of patients. . . . Among [those] in the second half of life—that is to say, over 35—there has not been one whose problem in the last resort was not that of finding a religious outlook on life.

> ⅋ CARL JUNG, quoted in *Time*, Feb. 14, 1955

When a man is freed of religion, he has a better chance to live a normal and wholesome life.

> ⅋ SIGMUND FREUD

Religion is a candle inside a multicolored lantern. Everyone looks through a particular color, but the candle is always there.

> ⅋ MOHAMMED NAGUIB, quoted in
> *News Summaries*, Dec. 31, 1953

Religion isn't yours firsthand until you doubt it right down to the ground.

> ⅋ FRANCIS B. SAYRE, dean, National Cathedral,
> Washington, D.C., quoted in *Life*, April 2, 1965

I'm going to take the moment to contemplate most of the Western religions. I'm looking for something soft on morality, generous with holidays, and with a very short initiation period.

> ⅋ TV character DAVID ADDISON in *Moonlighting*

If our faith delivers us from worry, then worry is an insult flung in the face of God.

>   ROBERT RUNCIE, Archbishop of Canterbury,
> address during April 1982 tour of Nigeria

I don't think man comes to faith firsthand except through despair or to knowledge of God except through doubt. It has to be a kind of watershed experience.

>   FRANCIS B. SAYRE, dean, National Cathedral,
> Washington, D.C., quoted in *Life*, April 2, 1965

Being religious means asking passionately the question of the meaning of our existence and being willing to receive answers, even if the answers hurt. [Such an idea of religion makes religion universally human, but it certainly differs from what is usually called religion.]

>   PAUL TILLICH, quoted in the
> *Saturday Evening Post*, June 13, 1958

The church is a whore, but she's our mother.

>   DANIEL and PHILIP BERRIGAN

God has no religion.

>   MAHATMA GANDHI (Similarly, "It is a mistake to suppose that
> God is only, or even chiefly, concerned with religion."
> [William Temple, Archbishop of Canterbury, quoted by
> R. V. C. Bodley, *In Search of Serenity*, 1939])

Religion is caught, not taught.

> ∞ W. R. INGE,
> dean of St. Paul's Cathedral, London

If men are so wicked with religion what would they be *without* it?

> ∞ BENJAMIN FRANKLIN

Religion is a feeble attempt to share the sense of God.

> ∞ JOHN DENVER

Extreme happiness invites religion almost as much as extreme misery.

> ∞ DODIE SMITH, *I Capture the Castle*, 1948

Got no religion. Tried a bunch of different religions. The churches are divided. Can't make up their minds and neither can I.

> ∞ BOB DYLAN

Religion is the vaccine of the imagination.

> ∞ NAPOLEON BONAPARTE, *The Mind of Napoleon*,
> ed. J. Christopher Herold, 1955

A religion that is small enough for our understanding would not be large enough for our needs.

       ARTHUR BALFOUR, as quoted in *Reader's Digest*, June 1958

Religion is a disease, but it is a noble disease.

       HERACLITUS

Most people have some form of religion—at least they know what church they're staying away from.

       JOHN ERSKINE, as quoted in *Reader's Digest*, Feb. 1942

Religion has not civilized man, man has civilized religion.

       ROBERT INGERSOLL

Religion is tending to degenerate into a decent formula wherewith to embellish a comfortable life.

       ALFRED NORTH WHITEHEAD

Religion, n. A daughter of Hope and Fear, explaining to Ignorance the nature of the Unknowable.

       AMBROSE BIERCE, *The Devil's Dictionary*

Religion enables us to ignore nothingness and get on with the jobs of life.

              ω   JOHN UPDIKE, *Self-Consciousness*, 1989

There are few among us who have not suffered from too early familiarity with the Bible and the *conceptions* of religion.

              ω   HAVELOCK ELLIS

Religion is a pill best swallowed without chewing.

         ω   Quoted without attribution by E. BERMAN in
Proverb Wit & Wisdom, 1997

The religions we call false were once true.

              ω   RALPH WALDO EMERSON

All religions issue Bibles against Satan, and say the most injurious things against him, but we never hear his side.

              ω   MARK TWAIN

To attempt to be religious without practicing a specific religion is as possible as attempting to speak without a specific language.

              ω   GEORGE SANTAYANA

God knew from all eternity that I was going to be Pope. You think he would have made me more photogenic.

                                       ප   POPE JOHN XXIII

Unitarianism is, in effect, the worst kind of atheism joined to the worst kind of Calvinism, like two asses tied tail to tail.

                         ප   SAMUEL TAYLOR COLERIDGE

Truth, in matters of religion, is simply the opinion that has survived.

                                  ප   OSCAR WILDE

The cosmos is a gigantic flywheel, making 10,000 revolutions a minute. Man is a sick fly taking a dizzy ride on it. Religion is the theory that the wheel was designed and set spinning to give him the ride.

                                  ප   H. L. MENCKEN

From the moment that a religion solicits the aid of philosophy its ruin is inevitable.

    ප   HEINRICH HEINE, *Religion and Philosophy in Germany*, 1835

Isn't religion just a cult that doesn't have to pay taxes, and shouldn't it pay them?

                          ප   BILL MAHER, *Does Anybody Have a Problem With That?*, 1996

Religion is what keeps the poor from murdering the rich.

         ₭ Napoleon Bonaparte

Religion is induced insanity.

       ₭ Madalyn Murray O'Hair, famous atheist

After coming into contact with a religious man I always feel I must wash my hands.

    ₭ Friedrich Nietzsche, *Ecce Homo*, "Why I Am a Destiny"

There is an enormous fatigue of trying to live without religion.

     ₭ Donald Barr, *Who Pushed Humpty Dumpty?* 1971

It is usually when men are at their most religious that they behave with the least sense and the greatest cruelty.

           ₭ Ilka Chase

Irreligious men are often better suited for godly missions.

          ₭ Hasidic Saying

Organized Christianity has probably done more to retard the ideals that were its founders' than any other agency in the world.

            ഔ   RICHARD LE GALLIENNE

You must believe in God in spite of what the clergy say.

            ഔ   BENJAMIN JOWETT

To all things clergic
I am allergic

            ഔ   Attributed to ALEXANDER WOOLCOTT

He represented what any minister will tell you is the bane of parish work: somebody who has got religion. It's as embarrassing to a cleric of sensibility as "poetry lovers" are to a poet.

            ഔ   PETER DE VRIES, *The Mackerel Plaza*, 1958

I am afraid the clergyman's God is often the head of the clerical profession.

            ഔ   WILLIAM R. INGE

There are three sexes—men, women, and clergymen.

            ഔ   SYDNEY SMITH

Priests are no more necessary to religion than politicians to patriotism.

                                                    ഔ   JOHN H. HOLMES

One of the proofs of the divinity of our gospel is that it has survived preaching.

                                            ഔ   WOODROW WILSON

The vices of the clergy are far less dangerous than their virtues.

                                       ഔ   EDWARD GIBBON

Religion is the idol of the mob; it adores everything it does not understand.

                                    ഔ   SOURCE UNKNOWN

Like a river dammed by its own ice, religion is held back by its congealed formulations.

                          ഔ   HARRY EMERSON FOSDICK

You catch religion, like you catch measles, from people—as much from what they are as from what they say.

                                    ഔ   LIONEL BLUE

A secular culture falsifies the world, for it ignores the highest level of significance in the drama of existence.

                            ℬ   BEN ZION BOKSER

There are moments in the lives of all men when you feel yourself completely belonging to something larger, nobler, more permanent than yourself. This experience is the religious experience.

                            ℬ   JOHN DEWEY

The great religions have as yet no common vocabulary or theological way of speaking, and this makes it necessary to take a stand within the framework of one religious tradition.

                          ℬ   WILLIAM JOHNSTON

Whatever else it is—let us be clear about that from the outset— religion is something we belong to, not something which belongs to us; something that has got hold of us, not something we have got hold of.

                          ℬ   RONALD A. KNOX

A religion without the element of mystery would not be a religion at all.

                          ℬ   EDWIN LEWIS

It is doubtless true that religion has been the world's psychiatrist throughout the centuries.

ත   DR. KARL MENNINGER

Religion is the metaphysics of the masses.

ත   ARTHUR SCHOPENHAUER

Religion is never devoid of emotion, any more than love is. It is not a defect of religion, but rather its glory, that it speaks always the language of feeling.

ත   D. E. TRUEBLOOD

Religion insofar as it is a source of consolation is a hindrance to true faith.

ත   SIMONE WEIL

A man who puts aside his religion because he is going into society is like one taking off his shoes because he is about to walk on thorns.

ත   RICHARD CECIL

Religion, like music, is not in need of defense, but rendition.

ත   HARRY EMERSON FOSDICK

We are for religion, against the religious.

                      ဢ   VICTOR HUGO

Religion is a monumental chapter in the history of human egotism.

      ဢ   WILLIAM JAMES, *The Varieties of Religious Experience*, 1958

Business is religion, and religion is business. The man who does not make a business of religion has a religious life of no force, and the man who does not make a religion of his business has a business life of no character.

                    ဢ   MALTBIE D. BABCOCK

The clergy have lost their hold. In America a man in trouble now goes to his doctor.

          ဢ   ALFRED NORTH WHITEHEAD

A theology—any theology—not based on a spiritual experience is mere panting—religious breathlessness.

              ဢ   LEONARD BOFF

I have only a small flickering light to guide me in the darkness of a thick forest. Up comes a theologian and blows it out.

                         ∞   DENIS DIDEROT

A priest friend of mine has cautioned me away from the standard God of our childhoods, who loves and guides you and then, if you are bad, roasts you: God as high school principal in a gray suit who never remembered your name but is always leafing unhappily through your files. If this is your God, maybe you need to blend in the influence of someone who is ever so slightly more amused by you, someone less anal. David Byrne is good, for instance. Gracie Allen is good. Mr. Rogers will work.

                         ∞   ANNE LAMOTT

Sign in a pastor's office: "Thank God it's Monday."

No man with any sense of humor ever founded a religion.

                         ∞   ROBERT INGERSOLL

Men of sense are really all of one religion. But men of sense never tell what it is.

                         ∞   FIRST EARL OF SHAFTESBURY

Theology is an attempt to explain a subject by men who do not understand it. The intent is not to tell the truth but to satisfy the questioner.

                               ɛꜱ   ELBERT HUBBARD, *The Philistines*, 1895

Man is the religious animal. He is the only religious animal. He is the only animal that has the True Religion—several of them.

                          ɛꜱ   MARK TWAIN, *Letters from the Earth*, 1962

We have just enough religion to make us hate, but not enough to make us love one another.

                                 ɛꜱ   JONATHAN SWIFT

Of all possible sexual perversions, religion is the only one to have ever been scientifically systematized.

                    ɛꜱ   LOUIS ARAGON, French poet, *Treatise on Style*, 1928

Religion converts despair, which destroys, into resignation, which submits.

                        ɛꜱ   THE COUNTESS OF BLESSINGTON

Religion is like music, one must have an ear for it. Some people have none at all.

                      ɛꜱ   CHARLOTTE MEW, in Penelope Fitzgerald's
                                Charlotte Mew and Her Friends, 1984

Why do people in churches seem like cheerful, brainless tourists on a packaged tour of the Absolute?

                    ANNIE DILLARD, *Teaching a Stone to Talk*, 1982

In some not altogether frivolous sense God needs to be liberated from theology. Theology is not a tabernacle to contain the One who is Ahead, but it is a sign on the way, and thus is provisional.

                    JOAN ARNOLD ROMERO

I doubt if we nuns are really as self-sacrificing as we must seem to be to you who live in the world. We don't give everything for nothing, you know. The mystery plays fair.

                    ELIZABETH GOUDGE, *Green Dolphin Street*, 1944

The question "Are we significant to God?" is the religious question. It always was, and it always will be.

                    SEBASTIAN MOORE

Sometimes we think of religion as taking all the joy out of life, but instead it is like finding buried treasure, like finding a perfect jewel.

                    REV. CHARLES L. ALLEN

No religion is a true religion that does not make men tingle to their finger tips with a sense of infinite hazard.

      ❧ WILLIAM ERNEST HOCKING

God is too large to be contained by any one religion.

      ❧ BUMPER STICKER observed in Boston, Massachusetts

Even if God did not exist, religion would still be holy and divine.

      ❧ CHARLES BAUDELAIRE

Most people think they have religion when they are troubled with dyspepsia.

      ❧ ROBERT INGERSOLL

Among medieval and modern philosophers anxious to establish the religious significance of God, an unfortunate habit has prevailed of paying him metaphysical compliments.

      ❧ ALFRED NORTH WHITEHEAD

I'm Jewish. I don't really follow the religion. Last time I was in temple, I was thirteen. I made my two grand. I got out of the business.

      ❧ MARK COHEN

You have these nuns beating your knuckles bloody and then telling you they were the sisters of God, and I felt like, "I don't want to meet your brother."

> ಸಂ JOE BOLSTER, as quoted by Bill Maher,
> *Does Anybody Have a Problem With That?*, 1996

Jews and Christians are different in a lot of ways. Some Christian people will actually have religious bumper stickers on their cars. Like "Jesus is King." "The Lord Saves." "Jews don't do that. You'll never see, "Honk if you Love Moses."

> ಸಂ GREGG ROGELL

Religions revolve madly around sexual questions.

> ಸಂ RÉMY DE GOURMONT

Religion is a bandage that man has invented to protect the soul made bloody by circumstance.

> ಸಂ THEODORE DREISER

Religion either makes men wise and virtuous, or it makes them set up false pretenses to both.

> ಸಂ WILLIAM HAZLITT, "On Religious
> Hypocrisy," *The Round Table*, 1817

Some years ago, when "the death of God" theology was a fad, I remember seeing a bumper sticker that read "My God is not dead; sorry about yours." I guess my bumper sticker reads "My God is not cruel; sorry about yours."

                                                      ᴓ   Rᴀʙʙɪ Hᴀʀᴏʟᴅ S. Kᴜsʜɴᴇʀ,
When Bad Things Happen to Good People, 1981

There's no reason to bring religion into it. I think we ought to have as great a regard for religion as we can, so as to keep it out of as many things as possible.

                ᴓ   Sᴇᴀɴ O'Cᴀsᴇʏ, *The Plough and the Stars*, 1926

Men despise religion. They hate it and are afraid it may be true.

                       ᴓ   Bʟᴀɪsᴇ Pᴀsᴄᴀʟ, *Pensées*, 1671

Religion is probably, after sex, the second oldest resource which human beings have available to them for blowing their minds.

                         ᴓ   Sᴜsᴀɴ Sᴏɴᴛᴀɢ, "The Pornographic
Imagination," in *Styles of Radical Will*, 1969

For a truly religious man, nothing is tragic.

                             ᴓ   Lᴜᴅᴡɪɢ Wɪᴛᴛɢᴇɴsᴛᴇɪɴ,
in *Personal Recollections*, ed. Rush Rhees, 1981

Religion consists in believing that everything which happens is extraordinarily important. It can never disappear from the world, precisely for that reason.

                                           ൟ   CESARE PAVESE

Religion, oh, just another of those numerous failures resulting from an attempt to popularize art.

                    ൟ   EZRA POUND, as quoted by Humphrey
Carpenter, *A Serious Character*, 1988

All outward forms of religion are almost useless, and are the causes of endless strife. . . . Believe there is a great power silently working all things for good, behave yourself and never mind the rest.

                 ൟ   BEATRIX POTTER, in *Journals, 1881–1897*, 1966

Not every religion has to have St. Augustine's attitude to sex. Whey even in our culture marriages are celebrated in a church, everyone present knows what is going to happen that night, but that doesn't prevent it from being a religious ceremony.

                          ൟ   LUDWIG WITTGENSTEIN,
Austrian philosopher, in conversation in 1943,
in *Personal Recollections*, ed. Rush Rhees, 1981

Randomness scares people. Religion is a way to explain randomness.

                                     ൟ   FRAN LEBOWITZ

In all religiousness there lurks the suspicion that we invented the story that God loves us.

                                          ℘ SEBASTIAN MOORE

In fact I'm always reading about the church, and about faith in general—precisely because I *lack* faith, and don't understand it. (I guess it's an emotional thing where you just say you give up, "I believe," and that's all. But what I just couldn't take about the church anymore, and still can't, is the hell, fire and damnation part. Get rid of that and I might be a good Catholic.)

             ℘ FRANK MCCOURT, as quoted by Ronald B. Shwartz
                  in *For the Love of Books: 115 Celebrated*
                 Writers on the Books They Love Most, 1999

In religion we believe only what we do not understand, except in the instance of an intelligible doctrine that contradicts an incomprehensible one. In that case we believe the former as a part of the latter.

                                         ℘ AMBROSE BIERCE

I find myself admiring more and more the Latin church, which for all its frequent astounding imbecilities has kept clearly before it the idea that religion is not a syllogism but a poem.

                                     ℘ H. L. MENCKEN

God and Prayer

&

If you talk to God, you are praying; if God talks to you, you have schizophrenia.

ఴ THOMAS SZASZ, *The Second Sin*, 1973

I rarely speak about God. To God, yes. I protest against Him. I shout at Him. But to open a discourse about the qualities of God, about the problems that God imposes, theodicy, no. And yet He is there, in silence, in filigree.

ఴ ELIE WIESEL, as quoted by George Plimpton, ed., *Writers at Work*, 1988

Father expected a good deal of God. He didn't actually accuse God of inefficiency, but when he prayed his tone was loud and angry, like that of a dissatisfied guest in a carelessly managed hotel.

ఴ CLARENCE DAY

What men usually ask of God when they pray is that two and two not make four.

ఴ Quoted without attribution by W. H. AUDEN and L. KRONENBERG, *The Faber Book of Aphorisms*, 1964

When praying, don't give God instructions. God listens to prayer, not advice.

                                               ⊗   EDWIN KEITH

I did not know we had ever quarreled.

               ⊗   HENRY DAVID THOREAU, on his deathbed,
when asked by his aunt if he had made his peace with God

Forgive, O Lord, my little jokes on Thee,
And I'll forgive Thy great big one on me.

                     ⊗   ROBERT FROST, "Cluster of Faith," 1962

I often pray, though I'm not really sure Anyone's listening; and I phrase it carefully, just in case He's literary.

                        ⊗   MIGNON MCLAUGHLIN,
The Complete Neurotic's Notebook, 1981

There is a great deal of skepticism in believers; and a good deal of belief in non-believers; the only question is where we decide to give our better energy. "Lord, I believe; help thou mine unbelief" may, and should, be prayed, two ways.

                            ⊗   CHARLES WILLIAMS

To pray is to ask that the laws of the universe be annulled on behalf of a single practitioner confessedly unworthy.

                 ⊗   AMBROSE BIERCE, *The Devil's Dictionary*, 1925

Prayer must never be answered: if it is, it ceases to be prayer
and becomes correspondence.

                                 ℅   OSCAR WILDE

It is not well for a man to pray cream and live skim milk.

                           ℅   HENRY WARD BEECHER

God punishes us mildly by ignoring our prayers and severely by
answering them.

                           ℅   RICHARD J. NEEDHAM

Office Prayer: Lord, Grant me the Serenity to accept the things I
cannot change, the Courage to change the things I can and the
Wisdom to hide the bodies of those people I had to kill because
they pissed me off.

                           ℅   SOURCE UNKNOWN

Don't pray when it rains if you don't pray when the sun shines.

                           ℅   SATCHELL PAIGE

The object of most prayers is to wangle an advantage on good
intentions.

                           ℅   ROBERT BRAULT

When we pray to God we must be seeking nothing—nothing.

              ဢ   SAINT FRANCIS OF ASSISI

Pray to God, but row toward the shore.

                    ဢ   RUSSIAN PROVERB

The doctrine of the material efficacy of prayer reduces the Creator to a cosmic bellhop of a not very bright or reliable kind.

                  ဢ   HERBERT J. MULLER

Dear God: You help strangers, so why not me?

                     ဢ   JEWISH SAYING

If your prayers were always answered, you'd have reason to doubt the wisdom of God.

                ဢ   SOURCE UNKNOWN

There is nothing in the world more dreary than a prayer that attempts to inform God of anything at all.

          ဢ   EDWARD N. WEST, former Subdean,
            Cathedral Church of St. John the Divine,
              New York City, to New York School of
                  Theology, Oct. 2, 1983

Don't bargain with God.

                ৰু   Yɪᴅᴅɪsʜ Pʀᴏᴠᴇʀʙ

"Give us this day our daily bread" is probably the most perfectly constructed and useful sentence ever set down in the English language.

            ৰু   P. J. Wɪɴɢᴀᴛᴇ, quoted in
the *Wall Street Journal*, Aug. 8, 1977

Prayer does not change God, but it changes him who prays.

            ৰু   Søʀᴇɴ Kɪᴇʀᴋᴇɢᴀᴀʀᴅ

Prayer by Politicians: "Teach us, O Lord, to utter words that are tender and gentle, for tomorrow we may have to eat them."

            ৰু   Sᴏᴜʀᴄᴇ Uɴᴋɴᴏᴡɴ

I've found that prayers work best when you have big players.

            ৰু   Legendary football coach Kɴᴜᴛᴇ Rᴏᴄᴋɴᴇ

"Dear God, please help me be the person my dog thinks I am."

     ৰু   Attributed to a member of the First Presbyterian Church,
Yuma, Arizona, as the best prayer he had ever heard

Prayers are little messages sent up to God at night to get a cheaper rate.

           ৪১   A child's definition as cited without attribution
by FRANK S. MEAD, *The Encyclopedia of Religious Quotations*, 1965

I never ask God to give me anything; I only ask him to put me where things are.

                                   ৪১   MEXICAN PROVERB

"Oh, God, if I were sure I were to die tonight I would repent at once." It is the commonest prayer in all languages.

           ৪১   SIR MATTHEW BARRIE, *Sentimental Tommy*, 1912

Of God and Man

ॐ

"Your money or your life." We know what to do when a burglar makes this demand of us, but not when God does.

                                ဢ   MIGNON MCLAUGHLIN,
The Complete Neurotic's Notebook, 1981

If God lived on earth, people would break his windows.

                                ဢ   YIDDISH PROVERB

God gives nothing to those who keep their arms crossed.

                                ဢ   WEST AFRICAN SAYING

If you want to give God a good laugh, tell him your plans.

                                ဢ   YIDDISH PROVERB

Your talent is God's gift to you. What you do with it is your gift back to God.

                                ဢ   LEO BUSCAGLIA

I do not feel obliged to believe that the same God who has endowed us with sense, reason, and intellect has intended us to forgo their use.

                                                        ઠ   GALILEO GALILEI

God can no more do without us than we can do without him.

                                                    ઠ   MEISTER ECKHART

In the nineteenth century the problem was that God is dead; in the twentieth century the problem is that man is dead.

                                                    ઠ   ERICH FROMM

It is not God who will save us, it is we who will save God—by battling, by creating, and by transmuting matter into spirit.

                                         ઠ   NIKOS KAZANTZAKIS

After God created the world, He made man and woman. Then, to keep the whole thing from collapsing, He invented humor.

                              ઠ   Attributed to "MORDILLO" by Bill Kelly

You come to God in many ways. A student I knew read the Summa of Thomas Aquinas, said "that's it," threw up his career, changed his religion and became a priest. Julian of Norwich, in the Middle Ages, had a bad dose of flu, ran a temperature and saw visions.

                                                    ઠ   LIONEL BLUE

A lot of people are willing to give God credit, but so few ever give Him cash.

          ɛ͡ɔ   Rᴇᴠ. Rᴏʙᴇʀᴛ E. Hᴀʀʀɪs, *Laugh with the Circuit Rider*

I never really look for anything. What God throws my way comes. I wake up in the morning and whichever way God turns my feet, I go.

          ɛ͡ɔ   Pᴇᴀʀʟ Bᴀɪʟᴇʏ

"I love God, father," she said haughtily. He took a quick look at her in the light of the candle burning on the floor—the hard old raisin eyes under the black shawl—another of the pious—like himself.

    "How do you know? Loving God isn't any different from loving a man—or a child. It's wanting to be with Him, to be near Him." He made a hopeless gesture with his hands. "It's wanting to protect Him from yourself."

          ɛ͡ɔ   Gʀᴀʜᴀᴍ Gʀᴇᴇɴᴇ, *The Power and the Glory*, 1961

If God were a poet or took poetry seriously or science for that matter, he would never have given man free will.

          ɛ͡ɔ   W. H. Aᴜᴅᴇɴ, "Squares and Oblongs," *Poets at Work*, 1948

A clear understanding of God makes one want to follow the direction of things, the direction of oneself.

          ɛ͡ɔ   Aɴᴅʀᴇ́ Gɪᴅᴇ, *The Journals of André Gide*, Vol. I, 1947

I believe more and more that God must not be judged on this earth. It is one of his sketches that has turned out badly.

      ह   VINCENT VAN GOGH, quoted in *The Rebel* by Albert Camus, 1956

How important the concept of God is, and how instead of valuing what has been given us, we with light hearts spurn it because of absurdities that have been attached to it.

      ह   LEO TOLSTOY, *Last Diaries*, 1960

The universe is merely a fleeting idea in God's mind—a pretty uncomfortable thought, particularly if you've just made a down payment on a house.

      ह   WOODY ALLEN

You are not obliged to put on evening clothes to meet God.

      ह   AUSTIN O'MALLEY

A pastor visited a family whose son had been killed in an automobile accident. He heard the mother rail out at him: "Where was your God when my boy was killed?" He quietly said, "The same place He was when His Son was killed."

      ह   ROGER LOVETTE

It may be that our role on this planet is not to worship God—but to create him.

      ह   ARTHUR C. CLARKE

I think God's going to come down and pull civilization over for speeding.

> ∾ STEVEN WRIGHT

Human beings are God's language.

> ∾ An unnamed Hasidic rabbi
> quoted by RABBI HAROLD S. KUSHNER,
> *When Bad Things Happen to Good People*, 1981

I find it interesting that the meanest life, the poorest existence, is attributed to God's will, but as human beings become more affluent, as their living standard and style begin to ascend the material scale, God descends the scale of responsibility at a commensurate speed.

> ∾ MAYA ANGELOU, *I Know Why the Caged Bird Sings*, 1969

Nobody has ever been able to understand why God preferred Abel's sacrifice to that of Cain.

> ∾ LEO SHESTOV, *All Things Are Possible*, 1905

I can't understand how all this can happen. It's enough to make one lose one's faith in God!

> ∾ EVA BRAUN, writing to a friend from
> Hitler's bunker during the seige and
> bombing of Berlin in April 1945

God's plan made a hopeful beginning,
But man spoiled his chances by sinning.
We trust that the story
Will end in God's glory
But at present the other side's winning.

> ᔕ ANONYMOUS limerick, quoted in
> the *New York Times Magazine*, 1946

When you knock, ask to see God—none of the servants.

> ᔕ HENRY DAVID THOREAU

Most people wish to serve God—but only in an advisory capacity.

> ᔕ ANONYMOUS

I've never been able to take sins of the flesh awfully seriously,
nor do I believe that God takes them terribly seriously.

> ᔕ JOHN UPDIKE, quoted in the *Kansas City Star*,
> Oct. 14, 1986

When you say a situation or a person is hopeless, you're
slamming the door in the face of God.

> REV. CHARLES L. ALLEN

It is not my business to think about myself. My business is to
think about God. It is for God to think about me.

> SIMONE WEIL, *Waiting for God*, 1951

It always strikes me, and it is very peculiar, that when we see the image of indescribable and unutterable desolation—of loneliness, of poverty and misery, the end of all things, or their extreme—then rises in our mind the thought of God.

         ເຈ VINCENT VAN GOGH,
Dear Theo: An Autobiography of Vincent van Gogh, 1937

In terms of greatness, the entire creation is to the Creator what a speck of dust is to the entire creation.

            ເຈ ANONYMOUS

I say to mankind, Be not curious about God. For I, who am curious about each, am not curious about God—I hear and behold God in every object, yet understand God not in the least.

       ເຈ WALT WHITMAN, *Leaves of Grass*

The more we understand individual things, the more we understand God.

             ເຈ SPINOZA

In his holy flirtation with the world, God occasionally drops a handkerchief. These handkerchiefs are called saints.

         ເຈ FREDERICK BUECHNER,
Wishful Thinking: A Theological ABC, 1973

A man without God is like a ship without a rudder.

> ஐ   Quoted without attribution by
> ALFRED ARMAN MONTAPART, *Distilled Wisdom*, 1964

I can see, and that is why I can be happy, in what you call the dark, but which to me is golden. I can see a God-made world, not a man-made world.

> ஐ   HELEN KELLER, replying to the question, "Can you
> see a world?" in 1955 documentary *The Unconquered*

Every happening, great and small, is a parable whereby God speaks to us, and the art of life is to get the message.

> ஐ   MALCOLM MUGGERIDGE, quoted
> in *News Summaries*, Dec. 31, 1978

I am a little pencil in the hand of a writing God who is sending a love letter to the world.

> ஐ   MOTHER TERESA, quoted in
> *News Summaries*, Sept. 1, 1982

What preoccupies us, then, is not God as a fact of nature, but as a fabrication useful for a God-fearing society. God himself becomes not a power but an image.

> ஐ   DANIEL J. BOORSTEIN, *The Image*, 1961

He who would be friends with God must remain alone or make the whole world his friend.

                 ℘   MAHATMA GANDHI

If there is a God, *since* there is a God, the human race is implicated in some terrible aboriginal calamity. It is out of joint with the purposes of its Creator.

    ℘   CARDINAL JOHN HENRY NEWMAN, *Apologia pro Vita Sua*, 1864

When I am operating, I feel the presence of God so real that I cannot tell where His skill ends and mine begins.

             ℘   Attributed to a famous surgeon

I have never been afflicted by the idea of God. I have never awakened in the middle of the night and said, without the idea of God my life would be meaningless.

                ℘   CLIFTON FADIMAN

We are in the 44th year of the Bomb. While it is certainly not proof, it is nevertheless Exhibit A of the grace of God that this little planet, Earth, is still here and that we continue our common lives on it.

             ℘   JAMES A. SANDERS

We speak of God as love, but are afraid to call God lover.

                                         ℘   SALLIE MCFAGUE

I have always believed in God, though I have my quarrels with Him. In the Jewish tradition, one may say no to God if it is on behalf of other people.

                                         ℘   ELIE WIESEL

Before God we are all equally wise and equally foolish.

                                         ℘   ALBERT EINSTEIN

Truth rests with God alone, and a little bit with me.

                                         ℘   YIDDISH PROVERB

What men call accident is God's own part.

                                         ℘   GAMALIEL BAILEY

We always keep God waiting while we admit more importunate suitors.

                                         ℘   MALCOLM DE CHAZAL

In a small house God has His corner, in a big house He has to stand in the hall.

                                         ℘   SWEDISH PROVERB

God, as some cynic has said, is always on the side which has the best football coach.

                                          ഇ   HEYWOOD BROUN

To most of us it would be very convenient if God were a rascal.

                                          ഇ   SOURCE UNKNOWN

I am ready to meet my Maker. Whether my Maker is prepared for the ordeal of meeting me is another matter.

                                        ഇ   WINSTON CHURCHILL

For several years I maintained public relations with the Almighty. But privately, I ceased to associate with him.

                                        ഇ   JEAN-PAUL SARTRE

Herein we see God's great mercy . . . for the slaughter was in all 5,517, *but ten of the enemy's side were slain to one of ours.*

                                        ഇ   NEHEMIAH WALLINGTON

If God were a necessary Being of Himself, He might almost seem to be made for the use and benefit of men.

                                        ഇ   JOHN TILLOTSON

God is dead, maybe; Neitzsche is dead, that's for sure.

                                  ℘   ANONYMOUS

The most haunting and courageous comment I have ever heard about the Almighty, more powerful than any of the heretical broadsides hurled by H. L. Mencken, Voltaire, Stendhal, or the relentless George Bernard Shaw, is this old saying of the Jews: "Dear God: If you forgive us, we will forgive you."

                                  ℘   LEO ROSTEN

The less theorizing you do about God, the more receptive you are to his inpouring.

                     ℘   GOETHE, *Wilhelm Meisters Lehrjahre*, 1796

If God really thinks well of the human race . . . why did he not proceed, as in Genesis, to create man at once? What was the point of the ichthyosaurs, dinosaurs, diplodochi, mastadons, and so on?

                              ℘   BERTRAND RUSSELL

There are times when thinking about God separates us from him.

                     ℘   SIMONE WEIL, *Waiting for God*, 1951

It may be that God finished His work of creating eons ago, and left the rest to us. Residual chaos, chance and mischance, things happening for no reason, will continue to be with us, the kind of evil that Milton Steinberg has called "the still unremoved edifice of God's creativity." In that case, we'll simply have to learn to live with it, sustained and comforted by the knowledge that the earthquake and the accident, like the murder and the robbery, are not the will of God, but represent that aspect of reality which stands independent of His will, and which angers and saddens God even as it angers and saddens us.

            ❦   RABBI HAROLD S. KUSHNER,
When Bad Things Happen to Good People, 1981

Those who turn to God for comfort may find comfort but I do not think they find God.

            ❦   MIGNON MCLAUGHLIN,
The Complete Neurotic's Notebook, 1981

God's contempt for human minds is evidenced by miracles. He judges them [human minds] unworthy of being drawn to Him by other means than those of stupefaction and the crudest modes of sensibility.

            ❦   PAUL VALÉRY, *Tel Quel*, 1941

Everyone is as God made him, and often a good deal worse.

            ❦   MIGUEL DE CERVANTES

There is hope for the future because God has a sense of humor, and we are funny to God.

                                          ∾   BILL COSBY

All the errors and incompetencies of the Creator reach their climax in man.

                                        ∾   H. L. MENCKEN

I cannot admit that any man born . . . has either the knowledge or authority to tell other men what God's purposes are.

                                 ∾   JUDGE BEN B. LINDSEY

If God helps those who help themselves, it is a bitter criticism of Him that He cruelly neglects those who for one reason or another cannot help themselves.

                              ∾   GEORGE JEAN NATHAN

We have no choice but to be guilty
God is unthinkable if we are innocent.

                            ∾   ARCHIBALD MACLEISH

God's gifts put man's best dreams to shame.

                     ∾   ELIZABETH BARRETT BROWNING

When he sees little kids sitting in the back seat of cars, in those car seats that have steering wheels, with grim expressions of concentration on their faces, clearly convinced that their efforts are causing the car to do whatever it is doing, he thinks of himself and his relationship with God: God who drives along silently, gently amused, in the real driver's seat.

                             ✑   ANNE LAMOTT

I met God. "What," he said, "you already?" "What," I said, "you still?"

              ✑   LAURA RIDING, in M. Brown and
A. O'Connor, *Hammer and Tongues*, 1986

The young do not need God, and the old cannot find Him.
             ✑   MIGNON MCLAUGHLIN,
The Complete Neurotic's Notebook, 1981

Those who never rebelled against God or at some point in their lives shaken their fists in the face of heaven, have never encountered God at all.

             ✑   CATHERINE MARSHALL, *Christy*, 1967

Logic is a game men play as cats play with balls of string, whereas reality is a game God plays with us.

                      ✑   HAROLD ORLANS

It isn't so urgent . . . whether you believe in God as whether he can believe in you. If you will conduct yourself in a manner that might encourage him to believe in you, the time may come when you feel that you should return the compliment.

        ɬ   LLOYD DOUGLAS, *Invitation to Live*, 1940

I had a thousand questions to ask God; but when I met him they all fled and didn't seem to matter.

        ɬ   CHRISTOPHER MORLEY, *Inward Ho!* 1923

He who created us without our help will not save us without our consent.

        ɬ   SAINT AUGUSTINE

If you want to see man at his worst, observe what he does to his fellow men in the name of God.

        ɬ   SOURCE UNKNOWN

God is indeed dead
He died of self-horror
when He saw the creature He had made
in His own image.

        ɬ   IRVING LAYTON, Canadian poet,
The Whole Bloody Bird, 1969

Have you read my No. 1 best-seller? (There will be a test.)

        ℰꙅ   GOD, purportedly quoted on a billboard
conceived by advertising executive Charlie Robb
of the Smith Agency in Fort Lauderdale, Florida

**I know God will not give me anything I can't handle. I just wish
that He didn't trust me so much.**

        ℰꙅ   MOTHER TERESA

Man is a dog's ideal of what God should be.

        ℰꙅ   ANDRÉ MALRAUX

**If God has at last died in our culture, he has not been buried.
For the casually religious, he lingers on like a fond old relative
who has been so expertly embalmed that we may prop him up
in the far corner of the living room and pretend the old fellow is
still with us. [We have even taken pains to bend his fallen mouth
into a benign and permissive smile . . . and that is a comfort. It
makes him so much *easier* to live with. . . .]**

        ℰꙅ   THEODORE ROSZAK, American social critic,
Where the Wasteland Ends, 1972

I pray hard, work hard and leave the rest to God.

        ℰꙅ   FLORENCE GRIFFITH JOYNER, gold medal Olympian
generally recognized as the world's fastest woman runner
until her untimely death in 1998 at the age of thirty-eight

When people cease to believe in God, they don't believe in nothing; they believe in anything.

           ∽ G. K. CHESTERTON

I tell myself that God gave my children many gifts—spirit, beauty, intelligence, the capacity to make friends and to inspire respect. There was only one gift he held back—length of life.

           ∽ ROSE KENNEDY

Decisions can take you out of God's will but never out of His reach.

           ∽ SOURCE UNKNOWN

When I think of God, my heart is so filled with joy that the notes fly off as from a spindle.

           ∽ JOSEPH HAYDN

I fear God, yet am not afraid of him.

           ∽ SIR THOMAS BROWNING
    (Similar: "Fear God, yes, but don't be afraid of Him."
       J. A. SPENDER, *The Comments of
        Bagshot*, second series), 1911

It is possible to be too big for God to use you but never too small for God to use you.

           ∽ ANONYMOUS

If we assume that man actually does resemble God, then we are forced into the impossible theory that God is a coward, an idiot and a bounder.

> ℂ H. L. MENCKEN, quoted by Benjamin
> De Casseres in *Mencken and Shaw*, 1930

A little girl repeating the twenty-third psalm said it this way: "The Lord is my shepherd, that's all I want."

> ℂ *Baraca-Philathea News*

Every child comes with the message that God is not yet discouraged of man.

> ℂ RABINDRANATH TAGORE

What makes God happy? Seeing a poor devil find a treasure and give it back.

> ℂ YIDDISH PROVERB

It is good enough to talk of God while we are sitting here after a nice breakfast and looking forward to a nicer luncheon, but how am I to talk of God to the millions who have to go without two meals a day? To them God can only appear as bread and butter.

> ℂ MAHATMA GANDHI

We could not seek God unless He was seeking us.

                                            ℘   THOMAS MERTON

I read the book of Job last night—I don't think God comes well out of it.

                   ℘   VIRGINIA WOOLF, *The Letters of Virginia Woolf,*
                                    Vol. II, 1912–22, 1975

I still have problems with God—or he has problems with me. Terrible problems. He is God and I am not.

                     ELIE WIESEL, quoted in *Civilization* magazine

What part of "Thou Shalt not . . ." didn't you understand?

                 ℘   GOD, purportedly quoted on a billboard
             conceived by advertising executive Charlie Robb
                of the Smith Agency in Fort Lauderdale, Florida

The Irreverent Side

&

How much reverence can you have for a Supreme Being who finds it necessary to include such phenomena as phlegm and tooth-decay in His divine system of Creation?

          ജ   JOSEPH HELLER, *Catch-22*, 1961

The worst thing you can say about him [God] is basically he's an underachiever.

          ജ   WOODY ALLEN, in the 1975 film *Love and Death*

I sometimes think that God in creating man somewhat overestimated His ability.

          ജ   OSCAR WILDE

God isn't so smart. He created forty-one types of parrots and nipples for men. I would have started with lasers, eight o'clock on day one.

          ജ   DAVID WARNER, as "Evil," in the 1981 film *Time Bandits*

The chicken probably came before the egg because it is hard to imagine God wanting to sit on an egg.

> ဢ SOURCE UNKNOWN, quoted by R. BYRNE,
> *The Best 637 Things Anybody Ever Said*, 1982

Which is it, is man one of God's blunders or is God one of man's?

> ဢ FRIEDRICH NIETZSCHE, *Twilight of the Idols*, 1889

All God's children are not beautiful. Most of God's children are, in fact, barely presentable.

> ဢ FRAN LEBOWITZ, *Metropolitan Life*, 1978

If the average man is made in God's image, then such a man as Beethoven or Aristotle is plainly superior to God.

> ဢ H. L. MENCKEN

I fear that one day I'll meet God, He'll sneeze, and I won't know what to say.

> ဢ RONNIE SHAKES, American comic
> (Similarly, "When God sneezed, I didn't know what to say."
> Henny Youngman, NBC TV, Aug. 28, 1986.)

Christ died for our sins. Dare we make His martyrdom meaningless by not committing them?

> ဢ JULES FEIFFER

Even in the valley of the shadow of death, two and two do not make six.

                ℘   LEO TOLSTOY on his deathbed,
when urged to embrace the Russian Orthodox Church

It is impossible to imagine the universe run by a wise, just and omnipotent God, but is quite easy to imagine it run by a board of gods. If such a board actually exists it operates precisely like the board of a corporation that is losing money.

                ℘   H. L. MENCKEN, *Minority Report*, 1956

If you give me a choice
between voting for
"God is dead"
or
"Everything
including evil is God's will,"
I would have to abstain.

                ℘   ROBERT HALE, as quoted by Louis
Cassels, *A Faith for Skeptics*, 1972

How odd
of God
To choose
The Jews.

        ℘   WILLIAM NORMAN EWER, *Week-end Book*, 1924

But not so odd
As those who choose
A Jewish God,
But spurn the Jews.

            ဢ CECIL BROWN, in reply to
verse by William Norman Ewer

Not Odd
of God
Goyim
Annoy 'im.

          ဢ Anonymous, quoted by LEO ROSTEN,
Leo Rosten's Book of Laughter, 1986

God was left out of the Constitution but was furnished a front seat on the coins of the country.

          ဢ MARK TWAIN, *Eruption*, 1940

I don't need to be born again. I got it right the first time.

          ဢ DENNIS MILLER

God, to whom, if he existed, I felt I should have nothing very polite to say.

          ဢ JOHN MORTIMER, *Clinging to the Wreckage*, 1982

Contractions are the physiological process wherein a woman's cervix is dilated preparatory to birth, through hours of excruciating pain. When you think about it, this is a highly inefficient system for what is supposedly a completely natural process. It is as if God actually made a mistake. It is as if every time you swallowed food, it caused a searing pain in the eye. Other notable mistakes by God: menstruation, nipples on men, the need to "wipe."

                     GENE WEINGARTEN, *The Hypochondriac's Guide to Life and Death*, 1998

If you see a blind man, kick him; why should you be kinder than God?

                     IRANIAN PROVERB

God pulled an all-nighter on the sixth day.

                     ANONYMOUS

Why do inclusive persons want to call God the Father "He/She" but seem perfectly content with calling the devil a "he"?

                     SOURCE UNKNOWN

God bless America, but God help Canada to put up with them!

                     ANONYMOUS

How come if God is so all-powerful and omnipotent that he has such a short name?

> ๛   NINA WEISMAN, age six, as quoted
> by Leonard Louis Levinson in
> *Bartlett's Unfamiliar Quotations*, 1971

In the first place, God made idiots. That was for practice. Then he made school boards.

> ๛   MARK TWAIN

Diane Keaton believes in God. But she also believes that the radio works because there are tiny people inside it.

> ๛   WOODY ALLEN

Atheism is a non-prophet organization.

> ๛   Source Unknown

There was an Old Man with a Beard
Who said: "I demand to be feared.
Address Me as God,
And love Me, you sod!"
And man did just that, which was weird.

> ๛   Limerick attributed to ROBERT WODDIS

God isn't dead, He's just screening his calls.

> ๛   CONTEMPORARY POSTCARD

If God had meant Wimbledon to be played in great weather, he would have put it in Acapulco.

    ℘   British tennis official, as quoted in *Newsweek*, July 4, 1977

How can one better magnify the Almighty than by sniggering with him at his little jokes, particularly the poorer ones.

    ℘   SAMUEL BECKETT, *Winnie, in Happy Days*, 1961

If God helped those who help themselves, those who help themselves wouldn't have to hire expensive lawyers.

    ℘   LEO ROSTEN

God is dead. But don't worry—the Virgin Mary is pregnant again.

    ℘   GRAFFITO, Los Angeles, 1981

Fuck all the asshole people who say, "God bless," and then don't bother to complete the sentence. Who they are, I haven't the slightest. But, if I were God, I would not honor such a request.

    ℘   GEORGE CARLIN

"Drop Kick Me Jesus Through the Goal Posts of Life."

    ℘   Title of country-and-western song

"Thou shalt not kill. Thou shall not commit adultery. Don't eat pork." I'm sorry, what was that last one? "Don't eat pork." God has spoken. Is that the word of God or is that pigs trying to out-smart everybody?

                                             ℘   JON STEWART

Making fun of born-again Christians is like hunting dairy cows with a high-powered rifle and scope.

                                             ℘   P. J. O'ROURKE

The problem with born-again Christians is that they are an even bigger pain the second time around.

                                             ℘   HERB CAEN

If I could just see a miracle. Just one miracle. If I could see a burning bush or the seas part or my uncle Sacha pick up a check.

                                             ℘   WOODY ALLEN

God made Adam before Eve because he didn't want any advice on the matter.

                                             ℘   PATRICK MURRAY

Between projects I go into the park and bite the grass and wail, "Why do you make me aware of the fact that I have to die one day?" God says, "Please, I have Chinese people yelling at me, I haven't time for this." I say all right. God is like a Jewish waiter, he has too many tables.

                                   ഔ   MEL BROOKS, quoted in *The Guardian*, 1984

When God created the world, He said it was good. That was His second mistake.

                                                    ഔ   JACK TANNER

God is not dead. He is alive and autographing Bibles today at Brentano's.

                                         ഔ   GRAFFITO, New York, 1979

The vengeful God is a stallion; in [Rev. Billy] Graham's hands, he is a gelding.

                            ഔ   MURRAY KEMPTON, *New York Post*, May 16, 1957

Let's all give God a great big hand.

                                             ഔ   REVEREND IKE

One half of the world does not believe in God, and the other half does not believe in me.

                                 ℰ   OSCAR WILDE

Our Heavenly Father invented man because he was disappointed in the monkey.

                                 ℰ   MARK TWAIN

If homosexuality were the normal way, God would have made Adam and Bruce.

                                 ℰ   ANITA BRYANT

God is for men and religion is for women.

                      ℰ   JOSEPH CONRAD, *Nostromo*, 1923

If Jesus were to come today, people would not even crucify him. They would ask him to dinner, and hear what he had to say, and make fun of him.

                               ℰ   THOMAS CARLYLE

Yes, I admit Jesus was Jewish—but only on his mother's side.

                               ℰ   ARCHIE BUNKER
                            from TV's *All in the Family*

Oh God, in the name of Thine only beloved Son, Jesus Christ, our Lord, let him phone me *now*.

                               ℰ   DOROTHY PARKER

The Bible says that the last thing God made was woman; He must have made her on a Saturday night—it shows fatigue.

                     ℰ   ALEXANDRE DUMAS PÈRE

It is a curious thing that God learned Greek when he wished to turn author(and that he did not learn it better.

                     ℰ   FRIEDRICH NIETZSCHE

Isn't God special?

                     ℰ   THE CHURCH LADY
                         from TV's *Saturday Night Live*

Obesity is a condition which proves that the Lord does not help those who help themselves and help themselves and help themselves.

                     ℰ   JULIAN BROWN

I don't know how God managed it. I'm having a terrible time.

            ℰ   JOHN HUSTON, film producer, while making *The Bible*

Don't question God, for He may reply: "If you're so anxious for answers, come up here."

    ⅋   Quoted from *Leo Rosten's Treasury of Jewish Quotations*, 1977

There, but for the grace of God, goes God.

    ⅋   WINSTON CHURCHILL, on Sir Stafford Cripps

If God made the body, and the body is dirty, the fault lies with the manufacturer.

    ⅋   LENNY BRUCE, in defense of his
stand-up comedy act
when he was arrested in San Francisco

Index

About the Editor

෫ා

Ronald B. Shwartz is a lawyer specializing in civil litigation and former editor of the *University of Chicago Law Review.* His most recent book is *For the Love of Books: 115 Celebrated Writers on the Books They Love Most* (Putnam, 1999). His essays and reviews have appeared in the *Wall Street Journal, The Nation, The American Spectator,* the *Los Angeles Times,* and other periodicals. In 1981 he was admitted to the National Book Critics Circle. His other books include *Men and Women Talk About Women and Men* (The Running Press, 1996) and *What Is Life?* (Citadel Press, 1995). Since 1986, Mr. Shwartz has been a partner with the Boston law firm of Goulston & Storrs. He is currently on a leave of absence and at work on a nonfiction book tentatively entitled *Where the Dreams Cross.*